CRAYOLA
FUN SCIENCE
CRAFTS

Rebecca Felix

LERNER PUBLICATIONS ◆ MINNEAPOLIS

The photographs in this book were created by Mighty Media, Inc.

Official Licensed Product
Lerner Publications Company
A division of Lerner Publishing Group, Inc.
241 First Avenue North
Minneapolis, MN 55401 USA

For reading levels and more information, look up this title at www.lernerbooks.com.

Main body text set in Mikado a 14/19.
Typeface provided by HVD Fonts.

Library of Congress Cataloging-in-Publication Data

Names: Felix, Rebecca, 1984– author.
Title: Crayola fun science crafts / by Rebecca Felix.
Description: Minneapolis : Lerner Publications, [2019] | Series: Colorful crayola crafts
Identifiers: LCCN 2018011475 (print) | LCCN 2018013631 (ebook) | ISBN 9781541512504 (eb pdf) | ISBN 9781541510982 (lb : alk. paper)
Subjects: LCSH: Handicraft—Juvenile literature. | Science projects—Juvenile literature. | Crayons—Juvenile literature.
Classification: LCC TT160 (ebook) | LCC TT160 .F45725 2019 (print) | DDC 745.5—dc23

LC record available at https://lccn.loc.gov/2018011475

Manufactured in the United States of America
1-43982-33996-9/25/2018

Contents

PAGE PLUS+

Scan QR codes throughout for step-by-step photos of each craft.

EXPERIMENT WITH ART SUPPLIES!

Are you a maker? You can be! Follow the steps to create cool science crafts.

Learn about the science concepts involved in each craft. Then experiment with colors and supplies to give each project a personal touch. Let's get creative with science!

Crafting Safety

▶ **Ask adults** for permission to use sharp tools.

▶ **Keep workspaces clean** and free of clutter.

▶ **Work carefully** with paints and glues. Protect your workspace before starting. Do not touch your face or eyes while using these materials. Wash your hands after use.

Science Crafting Tips

▶ **If a craft isn't turning out,** research why!

███ Learn about the science concepts behind art supplies' behavior, such as why clay hardens, colors mix, and more. Apply what you learn to complete your crafts!

▶ Science involves experimenting.

███ If you don't have a certain material, try something similar. Could tape work instead of glue? Markers instead of paint? Test it out!

███ Test out new methods too. Do you think a craft could be made simpler by switching steps? Try it!

COLOR CHEMISTRY RAINBOW

Mix art supplies and colors to create a rainbow with amazing hues!

Materials
- tempera paints
- plastic plates
- acrylic paints
- plastic knife
- oil pastels
- paintbrushes
- water
- small bowl
- spoon
- watercolor paints
- paper
- tape
- construction paper
- glue stick
- scissors

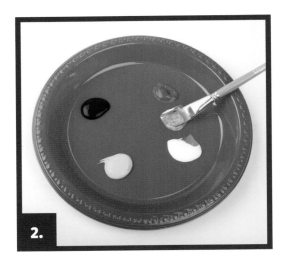

2.

1. Put blobs of tempera paint on a plastic plate. Fill a second plate with blobs of acrylic paints. Cut small pieces off oil pastels, and set them on another plate.

2. Use paintbrushes and a bit of water to mix colors on the tempera plate and then on the acrylic plate. Experiment! What color does mixing red and white paint create? What about red and blue? Blue and yellow?

Tip!
Before you get started, think about what will happen when you mix colors. Write down your predictions. After you've completed the experiment, see if you were right!

3. Crush and blend together oil pastel pieces using a spoon.

4. Next, mix mediums! Blend oil pastel pieces into tempera paint. Add streaks of watercolor paint to acrylic. What happens?

5. Use your color creations to paint a unique rainbow.

6. Tape two pieces of construction paper together. Glue your painting to the other side of the papers. Trim the construction paper to make a frame.

7. Use any leftover paint to make more rainbow works of art!

3.

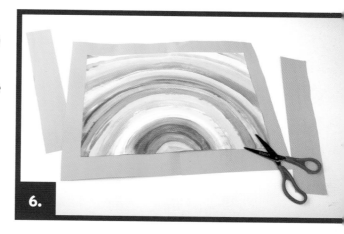

6.

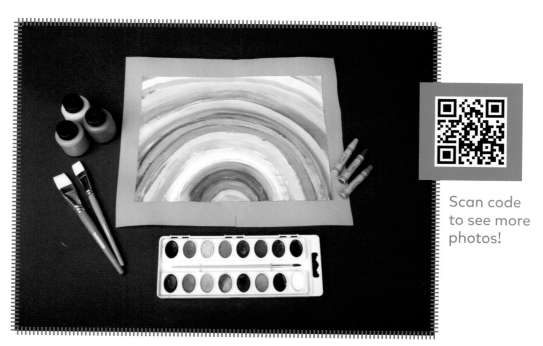

Scan code to see more photos!

HUBBLE SPACE PORTRAIT

The Hubble Space Telescope travels in space around Earth, taking photos of stars, planets, and galaxies. Craft artwork that looks like the Hubble's space snapshots!

Materials

- tempera paint
- glitter glue
- paintbrushes
- plastic plate
- scissors
- sponges
- paper towel
- plastic mat
- small bowl
- water
- pencil
- plastic bowls
- black construction paper
- washable school glue
- metallic markers

1. Mix different paint colors and glitter glues on a plastic plate.

2. Cut the sponges in half.

3. Place the paper towel on the mat, and fill the small bowl with water.

4. Dip a sponge in the water and then the paint and glue mixture. Dab the sponge on the paper towel to make patterns that look like galaxies and stars. Let the paper towel dry overnight.

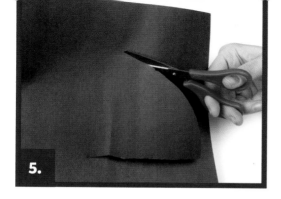

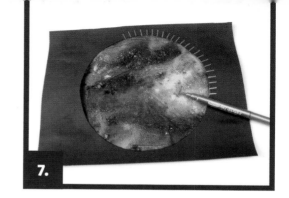

5. Trace the rim of a plastic bowl on black construction paper. Cut out the shape and discard it.

6. Add glue to the paper towel's corners, and glue the sheet of construction paper from step 5 on top. Trim any paper towel that sticks out from the paper.

7. Use metallic markers to draw lens details on the paper. Then make more Hubble snapshots and hang them on a wall!

DINOSAUR FOSSIL DIG

Construct dinosaur fossils and a mini archaeological dig!

Materials
- markers
- crayons
- paper
- tape
- shoebox with lid
- air-dry clay
- toothpicks
- coffee mug
- aquarium gravel, dirt, or sand
- plastic spoon
- plastic bowl
- large and small paintbrushes

1. Draw a picture of a dinosaur. Tape the drawing inside the shoebox lid.

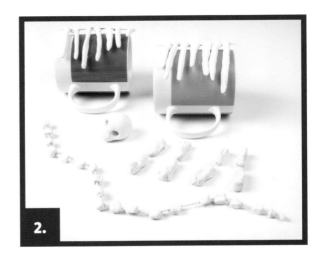

2. Make dinosaur bone fossils from clay! Look at your drawing. Think about the shapes of the creature's bones. Connect groups of bones, such as the spine or tail, using toothpicks. Place rib bones over a coffee mug to give them a curved shape. Allow all fossils to dry overnight.

3. Fill the shoebox with a bit of gravel, dirt, or sand. Add some of your fossils, and cover them with another layer of gravel, dirt, or sand. Repeat to make more layers.

4. It's time to go on a dig! Carefully uncover the fossils. Scoop the gravel, dirt, or sand into the bowl. Use the paintbrushes to reveal or brush the fossils clean.

5. After unearthing all the fossils, look at the dinosaur drawing to help you arrange the bones into a skeleton.

MOON FLIP-BOOK

Research the moon phases. Then watch a glowing moon go through its eight phases right in your hands!

Materials

- pencil
- bottle cap
- white construction paper
- scissors
- black construction paper
- paintbrushes
- glow-in-the-dark paint
- glue
- black paint
- stapler
- duct tape
- flashlight

4.

1. Trace the bottle cap on the white paper eight times. Cut out the shapes.

2. Cut out a black paper rectangle larger than the paper circles from step 1. Trace the rectangle on black paper 15 times. Cut out the shapes.

3. Paint one side of each circle with glow-in-the-dark paint. Let the paint dry.

4. Glue each circle near the right edge of a black rectangle.

5. Leave one circle all white for the full moon. Paint parts of the other circles black so their white areas match the seven other moon phases. Let the paint dry.

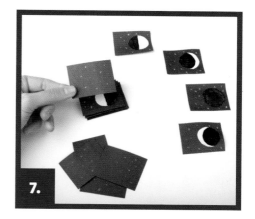

6. Use a paintbrush end to dot glow-in-the-dark paint around the moons as stars. Add stars to one side of all blank black rectangles too.

7. Stack the moons in phase order. Place a stars-only rectangle between each phase. This will make the stack thicker and easier to flip through. Staple the papers' left edges together to make a book.

8. Wrap a small piece of duct tape over the staples. Shine a flashlight on the book pages to charge the paint. Then turn out the lights and flip through your creation! Watch the moon complete its phases.

HOLOGRAM CUBE

Holograms are 3-D images made by lasers. But you can re-create their effect with plastic slides!

~~~~~~~~~~~~~~~~~~~~~~~~~~~~~~~

Materials
- scissors
- paper
- pencil
- plastic sheets or plastic clamshell container with flat surfaces
- markers
- rolling pin
- Model Magic
- plastic knife
- ruler
- glue

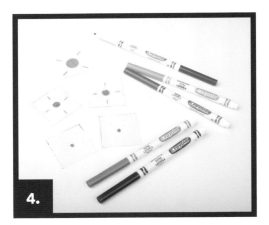
4.

1. Cut out a small paper square. Trace it five times on flat plastic, and cut out the squares. These are slides.

2. Draw a small, matching shape in the center of two slides.

3. In another color, draw the same shape but slightly larger on two more slides. Add extra lines or details near the shape.

4. In a third color, draw the same shape on the fifth slide but larger than it is on all other slides. Add extra lines or details near the shape.

5. Roll out some Model Magic. Use the knife and ruler to cut out four squares that are larger than the slides.

6. Glue the slides upright in one Model Magic square. Arrange them evenly apart and by the size of their shapes: smallest, medium, largest, medium, and smallest.

7. Carefully press a Model Magic square onto the top of the slides. Glue the other squares to the sides to make a cube. Allow it to dry overnight.

8. Hold your cube up to the light. The slides create a hologram!

Tip!
Be gentle when placing the slides into the Model Magic squares.

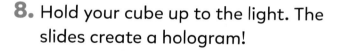

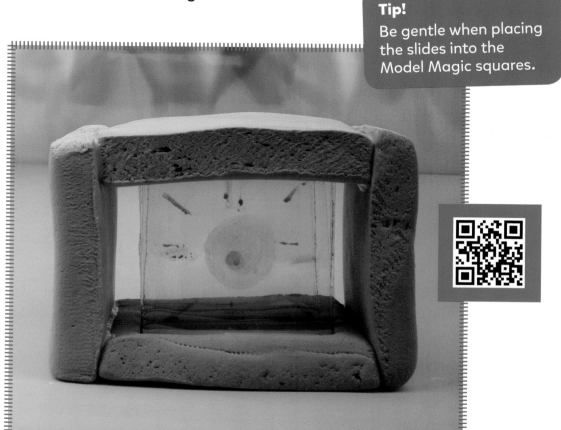

MYSTERY TEETH

Make a set of teeth for a mystery animal!
The animal's identity hides in its mouth.

Materials
- pencil
- notebook
- construction paper
- scissors
- shoebox lid
- ruler
- markers
- colorful duct tape
- air-dry clay
- glue

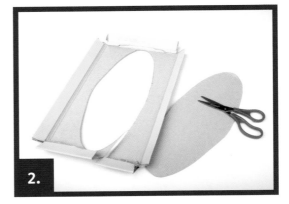
2.

1. Choose an animal and research its teeth. Write notes or draw shapes in a notebook.

2. Fold a sheet of construction paper in half. Draw the animal's mouth shape along the folded edge. Cut out the shape and unfold it. Then trace the shape on the shoebox lid and cut it out.

3.

3. Draw a line down the center of the cardboard cutout. Draw another line ½ inch (1.3 cm) away from either side of the line. Color between the lines with black marker.

4. Draw a tongue and color the animal's mouth. Write the animal's name inside the mouth.

5. Fold the cardboard along the edges of the black area.

6. Cover the other side of the cardboard in duct tape. Trim any extra tape. Fold pieces of tape in half, and tape two to the outside of the cardboard as handles.

7. Form teeth out of clay, and glue them inside the mouth. Let the teeth dry overnight.

8. Slip your fingers in the loops to make the animal mouth move. Have friends or family guess the animal. Open the mouth to reveal its name!

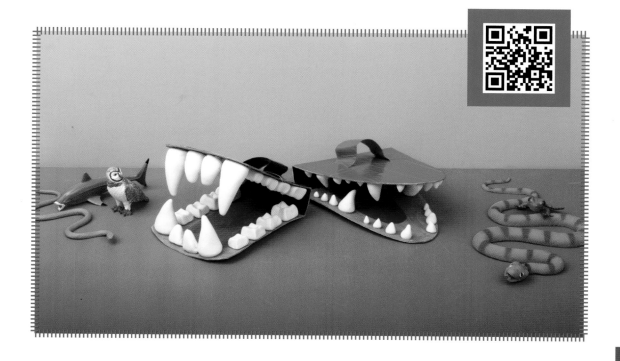

SHIPWRECK IN A BOTTLE

Make a mini ship and sink it in salt water. Don't look away!
Watch the water start to break down the ship in seconds.

Materials

- Model Magic
- rolling pin
- plastic knife
- air-dry clay
- small bowl of water
- scissors
- tissue paper
- toothpicks
- tape
- crayons
- markers
- glitter glue
- paint
- paintbrushes
- stickers
- plastic jar with screw-on lid
- water
- measuring spoon
- salt
- stirring spoon
- pencil
- notebook

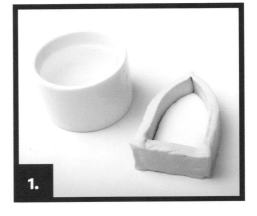

1.

2.

1. Form a ship bottom from Model Magic. Form ship sides from air-dry clay. Connect the pieces with water.

2. Cut small ship sails from tissue paper. Poke toothpicks through them as masts. Break a toothpick in half, and tape it together to make a longer mast.

3. Let the clay dry overnight.

4. Use crayons, markers, glitter glue, paint, and stickers to decorate the ship. Let the paint dry.

5. Fill the plastic jar ¾ full of water. Add a teaspoon of salt and stir to dissolve. Place the ship inside the jar, and screw on the lid tightly. Lay the jar on its side

4.

6. Watch what happens! Water breaks down even the toughest materials over time. Salt speeds up this process. What happens to your ship? Do the sails tear? Maybe the ship paint fades or chips. Observe the jar over the next hour. Record the results. Think about why some materials remain unchanged longer than others.

Tip!
A mast is a long pole that rises from the bottom of a ship or boat and supports the sails. Make sure the mast on your ship is sturdy!

SPACE ROVER

Design and build a mini rover, and then imagine it exploring space!

Materials

any combination of materials, such as:

- shoebox, small cardboard box, or container with lid
- paint
- paintbrushes
- glitter paint
- glitter glue
- school glue
- small metal objects like springs, washers, and nuts
- straws
- pencil
- plastic cups
- markers
- crayons
- pom-poms
- colorful duct tape
- old CDs or DVDs
- wooden wheels
- rubber bands
- paper towel tubes

1. Have an adult help you research NASA rovers online. Think about rover features that would be useful for exploring space.

2. Time to design! Gather items to help create the rover features you want to make.

3. Shoeboxes, small cardboard boxes, and plastic containers with lids make good materials for rover bases. Decorate your base using paint, glitter paint, glitter glue, and more.

4. Glue on washers, nuts, and other metal objects as buttons. Fill the holes in these objects with glitter glue.

Space Rover continued next page

5. Straws make great arms, antennae, or wires. Have an adult help you poke a hole in the base, and stick the straw inside the hole. Line the hole with glitter glue to hold the straw in place.

6. Glue on a plastic cup or other object as a control center cover.

7. Paint or draw details such as vents, meters, buttons, and stripes on your rover. Use markers, crayons, pom-poms, duct tape, and other materials.

8. Make rover wheels. Old CDs or DVDs and plastic caps or lids look good as wheels. Wooden craft wheels will allow your rover to actually move! Connect two wheels with a straw to make an axle. Place rubber bands at each straw end to keep the wheels on.

9. Duct tape the axles to the underside of the rover base.

10. Pretend your rover is taking off on a space mission! What do you imagine it will explore?

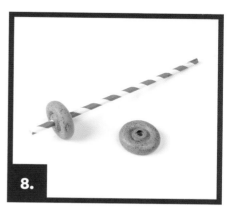

8.

RAIN FOREST IN A BOX

Discover how the sun reaches rain forest layers!

Materials

- pencil
- notebook
- shoebox with lid
- pencil
- scissors
- green duct tape
- construction paper
- clear tape
- glue
- brown and green tissue paper
- scissors
- markers
- flashlight

1. Have an adult help you research rain forest layers. Write down the layer names. Include some animals that live in each layer.

2. Divide the shoebox lid into four sections. Draw a small rectangle under each line. Have an adult help you cut out the shapes as well as one rectangle on the short side of the shoebox.

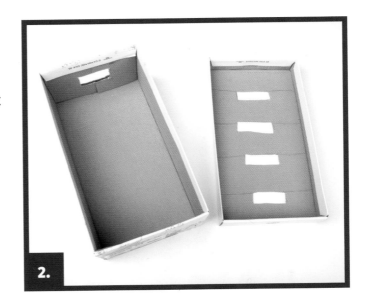

2.

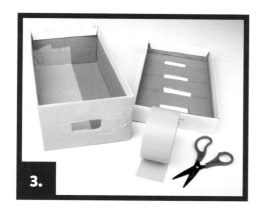

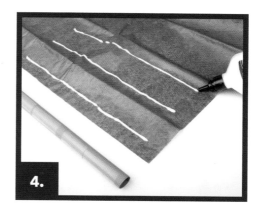

3. Cover the box and lid in green duct tape. Label each hole in the lid with a rain forest layer.

4. Roll a sheet of brown construction paper into a tube, and tape it together. Place lines of glue on brown tissue paper. Roll the paper around the tube, and trim the extra paper.

5. Cut the tube to fit into the shoebox as a tree. Repeat steps 4 and 5 to make more trees.

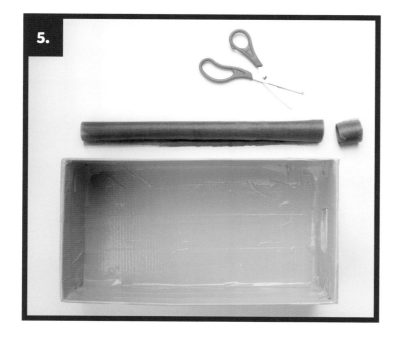

Rain Forest in a Box
continued next page

6.

6. Cut squares of brown tissue paper, and twist them into branches. Tape them to the trees.

7. Cut triangles of green tissue paper. Cut fringe along the shapes' edges to make leaves. Tape some leaves to the branches, and then tape the trees into the box.

8. Tape leftover leaves to the bottom of the box as shrubs and plants.

7.

8.

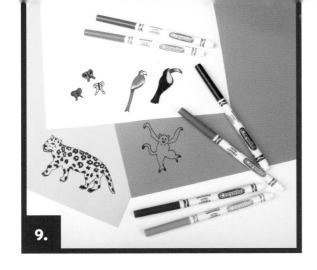

9. Draw and color animals for each rain forest layer on construction paper. Cut the animals out, and tape them to the trees inside the box.

10. Put the lid on the box, and stand it upright. Shine a flashlight in the top hole, and look through the lid. The flashlight acts as the sun shining above the top rain forest layer. How much light reaches the forest floor?

Get Creative!

Look at materials, steps, and craft photos. Are you missing some materials to re-create a craft? Would you have done the craft differently? Try it out!

Find new ways to make each project your own. Try swapping glitter glue for paint or a cardboard box with a plastic container. Make a hologram cube with many more slides or a rover that can float! With art supplies and some imagination, the possibilities are endless.

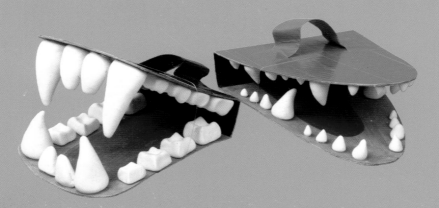

Glossary

acrylic: a chemical substance used to make fibers and paints

archaeological: dealing with the science of studying past life as shown by fossils and tools

axle: a pin, pole, or bar on or with which a wheel revolves

chemistry: the scientific study of substances, what they are composed of, and how they react with one another

dissolve: to seem to disappear when mixed with liquid

galaxies: very large groups of stars and planets

hologram: an image made by laser beams that looks as if it has depth and is three-dimensional

hues: colors, or types of colors

mediums: substances used to create a work of art

phases: stages of the moon's change in shape as it appears from Earth

predictions: guesses or expectations of what will happen in the future

rover: a space exploration vehicle

unique: unlike anything else

To Learn More

Books

Ardley, Neil. *101 Great Science Experiments*. New York: Dorling Kindersley, 2014.
Find 101 ideas for science projects and step-by-step instructions for each. Topics include electricity, sound, motion, and more!

Felix, Rebecca. *Mini Science Fun*. Minneapolis: Lerner Publications, 2017.
Create cool science crafts on a tiny scale! Learn to make little science labs, a mini working race car, and many other small wonders.

Miller, Rachel. *The 101 Coolest Simple Science Experiments*. Salem, MA: Page Street, 2016.
Discover a collection of simple science projects you can do indoors or outdoors! Each project has a meter to tell you how messy it will be, safety tips, and photos.

Websites

10 Science Crafts for Kids
http://101craftideas.com/kids-craft/82-science-crafts-for-kids/
Links and photos lead you to instructions on how to make all kinds of simple, colorful science creations!

Tiny Telescope
http://www.crayola.com/crafts/tiny-telescope-craft/
Craft a little telescope to wear around your neck. Keep it ready for your next space adventure!

Index